SOME MAJOR EVENTS IN WORLD WAR II

THE EUROPEAN THEATER

1939 SEPTEMBER—Germany invades Poland; Great Britain, France, Australia, & New Zealand declare war on Germany; Battle of the Atlantic begins. NOVEMBER—Russia invades Finland.

1940 APRIL—Germany invades Denmark & Norway. MAY—Germany invades Belgium, Luxembourg, & The Netherlands; British forces retreat to Dunkirk and escape to England. JUNE—Italy declares war on Britain & France; France surrenders to Germany. JULY—Battle of Britain begins. SEPTEMBER—Italy invades Egypt; Germany, Italy, & Japan form the Axis countries. OCTOBER—Italy invades Greece. NOVEMBER—Battle of Britain over. DECEMBER—Britain attacks Italy in North Africa.

1941 JANUARY—Allies take Tobruk. FEBRUARY—Rommel arrives at Tripoli. APRIL—Germany invades Greece & Yugoslavia. JUNE—Allies are in Syria; Germany invades Russia. JULY—Russia joins Allies. AUGUST—Germans capture Kiev. OCTOBER—Germany reaches Moscow. DECEMBER—Germans retreat from Moscow; Japan attacks Pearl Harbor; United States enters war against Axis nations.

1942 MAY—first British bomber attack on Cologne. JUNE—Germans take Tobruk. SEPTEMBER—Battle of Stalingrad begins. OCTOBER—Battle of El Alamein begins. NOVEMBER—Allies recapture Tobruk; Russians counterattack at Stalingrad.

1943 JANUARY—Allies take Tripoli. FEBRUARY—German troops at Stalingrad surrender. APRIL—revolt of Warsaw Ghetto Jews begins. MAY—German and Italian resistance in North Africa is over; their troops surrender in Tunisia; Warsaw Ghetto revolt is put down by Germany. JULY—allies invade Sicily; Mussolini put in prison. SEPTEMBER—Allies land in Italy; Italians surrender; Germans occupy Rome; Mussolini rescued by Germany. OCTOBER—Allies capture Naples; Italy declares war on Germany. NOVEMBER—Russians recapture Kiev.

1944 JANUARY—Allies land at Anzio. JUNE—Rome falls to Allies; Allies land in Normandy (D-Day). JULY—assassination attempt on Hitler fails. AUGUST—Allies land in southern France. SEPTEMBER—Brussels freed. OCTOBER—Athens liberated. DECEMBER—Battle of the Bulge.

1945 JANUARY—Russians free Warsaw. FEBRUARY—Dresden bombed. APRIL—Americans take Belsen and Buchenwald concentration camps; Russians free Vienna; Russians take over Berlin; Mussolini killed; Hitler commits suicide. MAY—Germany surrenders; Goering captured.

THE PACIFIC THEATER

1940 SEPTEMBER—Japan joins Axis nations Germany & Italy.

1941 APRIL—Russia & Japan sign neutrality pact. DECEMBER—Japanese launch attacks against Pearl Harbor, Hong Kong, the Philippines, & Malaya; United States and Allied nations declare war on Japan; China declares war on Japan, Germany, & Italy; Japan takes over Guam, Wake Island, & Hong Kong; Japan attacks Burma.

1942 JANUARY—Japan takes over Manila; Japan invades Dutch East Indies. FEBRUARY—Japan takes over Singapore; Battle of the Java Sea. APRIL—Japanese overrun Bataan. MAY—Japan takes Mandalay; Allied forces in Philippines surrender to Japan; Japan takes Corregidor; Battle of the Coral Sea. JUNE—Battle of Midway; Japan occupies Aleutian Islands. AUGUST—United States invades Guadalcanal in the Solomon Islands.

1943 FEBRUARY—Guadalcanal taken by U.S. Marines. MARCH—Japanese begin to retreat in China. APRIL—Yamamoto shot down by U.S. Force. MAY—U.S. troops take Aleutian Islands back from Japan. JUNE—Allied troops land in New Guinea. NOVEMBER—U.S. Marines invade Bougainville & Tarawa.

1944 FEBRUARY—Truk liberated. JUNE—Saipan attacked by United States. JULY—battle for Guam begins. OCTOBER—U.S. troops invade Philippines; Battle of Leyte Gulf won by Allies.

1945 JANUARY—Luzon taken; Burma Road won back. MARCH—Iwo Jima freed. APRIL—Okinawa attacked by U.S. troops; President Franklin Roosevelt dies; Harry S. Truman becomes president. JUNE—United States takes Okinawa. AUGUST—atomic bomb dropped on Hiroshima; Russia declares war on Japan; atomic bomb dropped on Nagasaki. SEPTEMBER—Japan surrenders.

WORLD AT WAR

Pearl Harbor

WORLD AT WAR

Pearl Harbor

By G. C. Skipper

Consultant:
Professor Robert L. Messer, Ph.D.
Department of History
University of Illinois at Chicago

CHILDRENS PRESS, CHICAGO

Japanese two-man submarines like this one took part in the attack on Pearl Harbor.

There are some you can never thank or love enough . . .

For my wife, Ann, whose exhausting research and inexhaustible love made this book and this series possible.

FRONTISPIECE:
Stunned sailors watch as fuel tanks explode at the wrecked seaplane base at Kaneohe Bay on the east coast of Oahu.

Library of Congress Cataloging in Publication Data

Skipper, G. C.
   Pearl Harbor.

   (World at war)
   Includes index.
   Summary: Describes the Japanese surprise attack on the United States naval base at Pearl Harbor, which resulted in the deaths of more than 2,000 American officers and servicemen and an immediate declaration of war on Japan.
   1. Pearl Harbor, Attack on, 1941—Juvenile literature. [1. Pearl Harbor, Attack on, 1941. 2. World War, 1939–1945—Hawaii]
I. Title. II. Series.
D767.92.S56 1983   940.54'26   83-6569
ISBN 0-516-04774-4

PROJECT EDITOR
Joan Downing

CREATIVE DIRECTOR
Margrit Fiddle

Night covered the Pacific Ocean like a heavy black blanket. Nothing broke the stillness except for tiny whispering ripples. Then something stirred with a quiet swooshing sound. The surface of the water broke. In the darkness a Japanese submarine, dripping like a monster from the deep, rose and bobbed in the great sea.

With a loud clang, a hatch opened. A Japanese submariner scrambled out and gazed toward a distant shoreline. The island before him glittered with light. He could see the glowing neon signs of restaurants and night clubs. He could hear the faint sounds of jazz music. American music.

Tomorrow, the man thought. *Tomorrow*.

Only a short while before the Japanese attack, these United States bombers were flying in formation over beautiful Honolulu, only a few miles from Pearl Harbor.

It was Saturday, December 6, 1941. The music drifting through the night came from the island of Oahu. For more than four decades, Oahu and the other Hawaiian Islands had been a territorial possession of the United States. (Hawaii didn't become a state until 1959.) Oahu's Pearl Harbor was a key naval base for the United States Pacific Fleet. About one hundred ships were anchored at Pearl Harbor—exposed, all but unguarded, and almost completely vulnerable.

These Japanese carriers were two hundred miles from Oahu as they waited to unleash the planes that would attack Pearl Harbor.

By the next morning, a Japanese task force of two battleships, six aircraft carriers, and assorted surface vessels and submarines was positioned two hundred miles from Oahu. From that distance, the aircraft on the carriers could easily reach the island. When the planes attacked, the United States would be plunged into war with Japan.

Japanese destroyers patrolled the South China Sea
only a few weeks before the attack on Pearl Harbor.

For several years before the attack on Pearl Harbor, the Japanese had been trying to extend their power. They believed in *Hakko Ichiu,* which means "bringing the eight corners of the world under one roof." Japan's destiny, they felt, was to be leader of all Asia.

The Japanese had been waging war with China since 1937. They had controlled Korea since 1910. When they invaded southern French Indochina (now southern Vietnam and Cambodia) in July of 1941, the United States immediately cut off sales of metal ores and oil to Japan. This was an effort to stop Japan from taking over other Asian countries.

Above: Japanese
troops cheer as
Nanking, the
Chinese capital
city, surrenders
in December, 1937.
Left: A baby
cries in pain and
terror amid the
ruins of a train
station in
Shanghai, China,
just after a
bombing raid
by the Japanese
in September, 1937.

In the months before the attack on United States bases in the Pacific, these young Japanese men trained rigorously for service in their country's air forces.

To the Japanese, the United States embargo meant there would have to be a war. Japan had no oil or metal ores of her own. She looked greedily at other Asian countries that had abundant resources, with conquest in mind.

At the time, the American public did not know just how close their country was to war with Japan. But some members of the United States government knew that it was just a matter of time. No one knew, however, exactly where the Japanese would attack.

Several factors prevented the American command from anticipating the surprise attack at Pearl Harbor. Even though the Americans had broken the secret Japanese diplomatic code, the decoded messages were closely guarded. People in important positions—such as Admiral Husband Kimmel and General Walter Short, the navy and army commanders at Pearl Harbor—never received the valuable information in them. Also, because of the economic depression carried over from the 1930s, there was little money for new equipment and more servicemen. Since Pearl Harbor was so shallow,

These planes, lined up wingtip to wingtip at Hickam Field near Pearl Harbor, were easy targets for Japanese bombs.

the American command felt that underwater torpedoes could not be used against ships there. Finally, the Americans felt that Japanese equipment and servicemen were inferior to their American counterparts.

However, the Americans did worry that sabotage was likely at Pearl Harbor. To keep an eye on things, the commanders grouped ships closely together in the harbor to keep them safe from submarines. Airplanes on the island were lined up wingtip to wingtip so that all could be watched by a few men. This sort of thinking was to result in disaster. The ships and planes crammed together made perfect sitting targets.

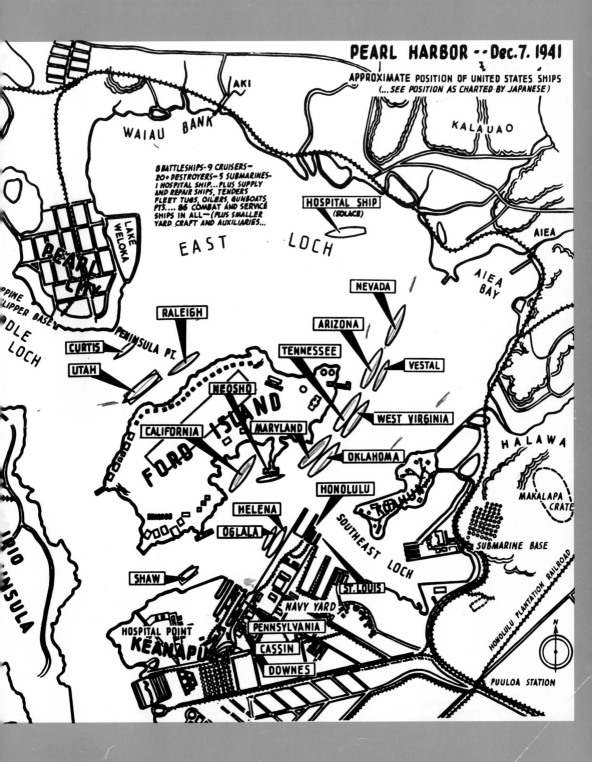

Japanese Minister of War General Hideki Tojo (in the uniform with high boots near the center of the photo) is shown drinking a toast to the Axis Pact (an alliance with Germany and Italy) that was signed in October, 1940.

Even though Japanese and American diplomats were still trying to negotiate a treaty late in 1941, General Hideki Tojo, the Japanese minister of war, began to plan for a full-scale war. Admiral Isoruku Yamamoto, the commander-in-chief of the Japanese Imperial Navy, drew up the plans to attack Pearl Harbor. He ordered Vice Admiral Chuichi Nagumo to execute them. Nagumo did so, to perfection.

These Japanese dive bombers were warming up on a carrier before taking off to attack Pearl Harbor.

On Sunday morning, December 7, 1941, the first of two waves of aircraft, about 180 planes, roared off the decks of the Japanese carriers north of Oahu. The noise from their engines was deafening. The Japanese airmen and sailors on the decks cheered as the planes zoomed off. The planes grouped together and headed for Pearl Harbor.

This Japanese navy pilot is shown as he prepared to take part in the Pearl Harbor raid. The pilots wore life jackets in case they were shot down over the Pacific.

The Japanese plan had two parts. The most important target was "Battleship Row," where the most deadly of the United States ships were anchored. Torpedo planes, dive bombers, and high-level bombers were to attack the ships there. The airplanes at the two main airfields were the second important target.

At Pearl Harbor, early church bells had just begun to ring. Some servicemen were still sleeping soundly. Others were making their way to breakfast. Things were so peaceful that two thirds of the antiaircraft guns aboard the ships in the harbor were unmanned. Not even the antiaircraft gun batteries on the island were ready. Of thirty-one such batteries, only four were in position to repulse an enemy attack. And those four had no ammunition at hand—the gunners had turned in their live shells after their last practice.

Attacking Japanese planes (circled) at Pearl Harbor on the morning of December 7, 1941.

The Japanese planes had left their carriers at 7:49 A.M. When they reached the islands with no resistance, the pilots radioed their carriers, "*Tora! Tora! Tora!*" (Tiger! Tiger! Tiger!), meaning the attack was a surprise. At 7:55 A.M., the Sunday morning quiet of Pearl Harbor was ripped apart when the first Japanese bomb dropped.

This aerial view of Pearl Harbor was taken from one of the Japanese planes during the attack.

The wave of enemy aircraft split up. Some swooped down on the harbor itself. Others headed for the nearby airfields. At first, the Americans thought an earthquake had hit. The island rumbled and shook from exploding bombs. Then, overhead, came the whine of enemy aircraft. Machine-gun fire spit angrily toward the ground.

This car, with its civilian driver inside, was strafed by bullets from a Japanese plane.

A few soldiers who had been caught outside looked up in surprise. For a moment they stood gaping. They couldn't believe what they were seeing. Japanese aircraft were coming in so low the Americans could see the goggles on the pilot's faces. Then bullets from the planes began to tattoo the earth, kicking up dust and dirt, slamming and smacking into walls and crashing through windows. Some of the American soldiers dropped, cut down by the gunfire.

Wheeler Field, shown in this Japanese photo, was the first target to be hit during the attack.

A few minutes into the attack, this shocking message was sent to the United States:

AIR RAID, PEARL HARBOR—THIS IS NO DRILL!

The enemy planes attacked like a flock of wild predator birds. They bombed and strafed the military planes lined up on the airfields. The planes on the ground began to blow up in a chain reaction. Horrible explosions rocked nearby barracks. Flames shot up everywhere.

The barracks and hangars at Hickam Field are shown here as they burned after the Japanese bombing raid. The B-17 bomber in the foreground escaped the attack.

Within the first few minutes of the sneak attack, most of the United States aircraft on the ground were in a shambles, useless heaps of torn and melting metal.

Along Battleship Row, seven great United States battleships lay at anchor. Four were inside the harbor and two were outside. Another ship, the *Pennsylvania*, was in drydock.

Hangars, planes, and other vehicles at Hickam Field were useless heaps of torn and melting metal after the attack.

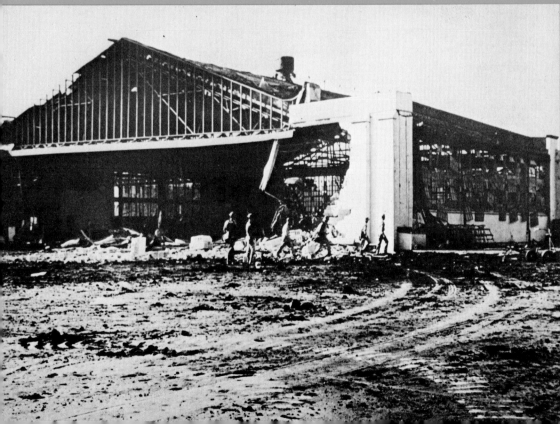

A small boat goes to the rescue of a seaman from the burning *West Virginia*.

"Fire!" yelled a Japanese pilot. "Do it now!"

The belly of his plane leveled out near the water. Suddenly, short-run torpedoes screamed out of the plane, slapped into the water, and sliced toward the battleships. These torpedoes—which United States intelligence claimed the Japanese did not possess—had wooden fins specially designed for an attack in shallow water.

The torpedo bombers, after dropping their deadly loads, pulled up sharply and fled back into the clouds. Meanwhile, high-level bombers and dive bombers poured out of the sky, dropping everything they had on the ships below in Pearl Harbor.

Suddenly, the battleship *West Virginia* was hit; it sank just a few minutes after the attack began.

As ruptured fuel tanks from a sunken ship send up a black column of
smoke (left), a tugboat (right) and other small boats search for
survivors from the capsized *Oklahoma* (center background) and other ships.

Then the battleship *Oklahoma* lurched in the
water. Within minutes, three torpedoes slammed
into her. The only possible order was given:
Abandon ship! American sailors leaped into the
water, trying desperately to swim to other ships
or to shore. More than four hundred men were
trapped inside the *Oklahoma* as she slowly began
to go down. The great ship finally capsized in
the mud at the bottom of the harbor.

Torpedoes found the *Utah*, a former battleship
that was being used as a target ship. The mighty
Utah seemed to wrench in the water as if it were
twisted by the hand of a cruel giant.

Soon the harbor's water became coated with
oil. Sailors trying to swim toward shore were
caught in the horrible slime. As the ships began
to explode, flames leaped down and ignited the
oil. A wave of fire raced across the water,
burning sailors to death.

At 8:12 A.M. the *Utah* rolled over. Part of the
ship slid below the waterline. The rest protruded
into the air. Men trapped inside beat frantically
on the hull—but no one could get to them.

No one could get to the men trapped in the hull of the sunken battleship *Utah*.

Crewmen struggle to bring the flames on the *Nevada* under control.

In the confusion, the damaged battleship *Nevada* made a desperate break for safety. She shoved through the harbor while sailors cheered her on. Her crew thought she might have a chance if she could reach open water. But Japanese submarines were waiting outside the harbor.

As the *Nevada* moved toward the sea, six bombs hit her. A few minutes later, the ship burst into flames. While crewman struggled to bring the fires under control, tugboats steamed to her rescue. They managed to haul the *Nevada* to the beach, but the damage had been done.

Meanwhile, Japanese torpedo planes screamed down on the battleship *Arizona.* On the planes' first sweep, the torpedoes slicked through the water, missing the great ship. The enemy aircraft came back—and this time five bombs slammed into the *Arizona.*

The ship burst into flames. The fire raged out of control, sweeping along decks, pouring down hatches, and licking up the sides of the ship. Sailors screamed as they were caught in the flames. Then the fire hit the black gunpowder stored on the ship.

The *Arizona* exploded. The huge ship broke into two pieces that plunged into the mud of the harbor. Thick black smoke, sliced by the bright colors of raging fires, marked the wreckage. As American sailors on the other ships watched the horrible sight, they knew the fifteen hundred men aboard had no chance of survival. The bodies of the men who died on the *Arizona* were never recovered.

Above: The U.S.S. *Arizona*, burning furiously, explodes and breaks in two before plunging into the mud of Pearl Harbor.
Below: The ruined remains of the *Arizona* as she looked three days later.

As the destruction of the ships in Pearl Harbor continued, more and more sailors leaped overboard into the flaming oily water. Many who jumped never made it to shore.

Even civilians were not to escape the attack. A Japanese bomb accidentally hit the city of Honolulu, killing nearly seventy civilians. People all over Hawaii were dazed with terror. The peace of their sunny Sunday had been shattered by death and destruction.

These residents of the outskirts of Honolulu, puzzled by the roar of diving Japanese planes, were not sure what to do. Some just stood still and listened; some looked toward the sky; and some ran.

Black puffs from exploding American antiaircraft guns dot the dense cloud of black smoke that rises from the burning battleship *Arizona*.

When a second wave of planes attacked, the initial confusion of the American servicemen changed to anger—anger at an enemy who dared to strike with such brutal surprise. Men ran toward armories where rifles and ammunition were stored. Others sought out the few undamaged aircraft and climbed into the cockpits.

The American planes roared upward to meet the Japanese attackers. Antiaircraft guns on ships and on land swiveled and cranked skyward. Those who manned them were determined to blast the enemy out of the sky.

Americans discovered that one Japanese midget submarine had sneaked into the harbor itself. They dropped depth charges and opened fire on its conning tower. The sub never came up again. An hour before the attack, a destroyer had sunk another sub outside the harbor, but a report of the incident had been more or less ignored until after the attack had begun.

As American guns barked skyward, some Japanese aircraft plunged seaward, trailing smoke; others flew away toward the open sea.

Pearl Harbor was pounded with bombs and torpedoes and strafed by bullets from 7:55 until 9:45 A.M. Then the Japanese planes turned and roared away. They simply vanished, as suddenly as they had appeared.

This Japanese midget submarine was beached during the attack.

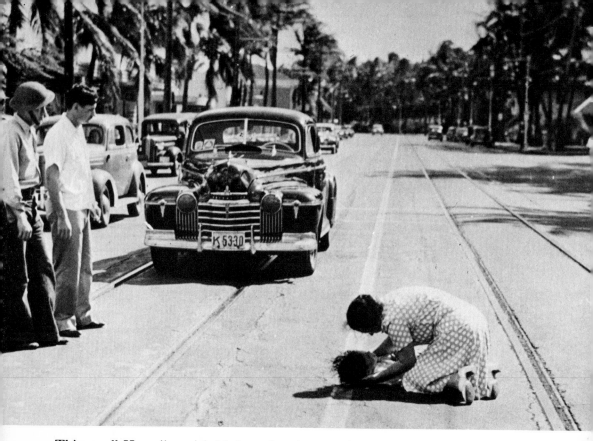

This small Hawaiian girl, hit by a frantic motorist, was one of the many civilian casualties of the panic caused by the Japanese raid on Pearl Harbor.

The noise of the guns and bombs and torpedoes was gone. But Pearl Harbor was not reposing in silence. Everywhere were the sounds of destruction. Everywhere was the crackling of burning fires. Everywhere voices shouted orders, sirens wailed, and injured men cried out for help. Others were so badly wounded that they could do nothing but moan and wait.

Some made no sound at all.

Grim-faced emergency first-aid workers help the wounded outside a
bombed school in Honolulu on the morning of December 7, 1941.

The battleships *Maryland* (above) and *California* (opposite) were badly damaged during the Japanese raid.

The attack on Pearl Harbor resulted in the deaths of 2,403 American officers and fighting men. A total of 1,178 were wounded. The Japanese had sunk the battleships *Arizona*, *West Virginia*, and *Oklahoma*. Beached and sinking was the *Nevada*. Damaged badly were the *Pennsylvania*, *California*, *Maryland*, and *Tennessee*.

The Japanese had sunk the destroyers *Cassin,* *Downes,* and *Shaw.* They also had sunk the target ship *Utah* and the minelayer *Oglala.*

The attack had damaged the cruisers *Helena,* *Honolulu,* and *Raleigh*; crippled the seaplane tender *Curtiss*; and slammed the repair ship *Vestal* against the beach, where it lay sinking.

But as the Japanese aircraft turned away from Pearl Harbor and headed for their aircraft carriers waiting out at sea, a few in their ranks also were missing.

A total of twenty-nine Japanese aircraft never returned to the carriers. And all five Japanese midget submarines used in the attack were gone.

The ruined destroyer *Downes* was struck by Japanese bombs as she lay in drydock.

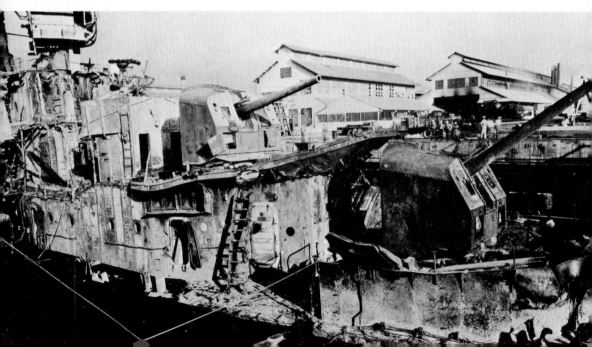

Only hours after the treacherous attack by the Japanese, President
Franklin Delano Roosevelt, during one of his most famous speeches,
declared war against Japan.

Less than twenty-four hours after the Japanese
attack began, President Franklin D. Roosevelt
addressed the United States Congress. His
famous "Day of Infamy" speech was carried live
by radio into homes and working places across
America. Congress immediately declared war
on Japan.

The attack on Pearl Harbor generated a spate of war songs in the United States. One of them was "We'll Always Remember Pearl Harbor," by Alfred Bryan, Willie Haskin, and Gerald Marks.

Americans were stunned, outraged, saddened, and angered by the sneak attack. "Remember Pearl Harbor!" became a popular slogan that rallied the nation. The United States reacted with all the strength and determination its people possessed. Major shake-ups occurred throughout the top ranks of the United States Navy. Everyone was determined that such a surprise attack would never happen again.

Even though the destruction was monumental, most of the ships caught in Pearl Harbor that day were not lost.

In drydock at the Pearl Harbor navy yard in February, 1942, the U.S.S. *Downes* (left) and the U.S.S. *Cassin* (right) were being readied for refloating.

The *Pennsylvania* was the first ship to be repaired. The *Oklahoma* and *West Virginia* were the last, sent to sea more than two years later.

Only the *Arizona* never rose; after the war, a memorial was erected over the sunken ship and the bodies it holds.

The other ships all went to work, met the Japanese enemy, and helped to defeat him four long years later.

The U.S.S. *Arizona* Memorial at Pearl Harbor was erected over the sunken ship on which fifteen hundred men on board died during the December 7, 1941 attack by the Japanese.

Index

Page numbers in boldface type indicate illustrations.

About the Author

A native of Alabama, G.C. Skipper has traveled throughout the world, including Jamaica, Haiti, India, Argentina, the Bahamas, and Mexico. He has written several other children's books as well as an adult novel. Mr. Skipper has also published numerous articles in national magazines. He is now working on his second adult novel. Mr. Skipper and his family live in Glenside, Pennsylvania, a suburb of Philadelphia.